This book belongs to

_____

This book is dedicated to my children - Mikey, Kobe, and Jojo.

Copyright © 2023 Grow Grit Press LLC. All rights reserved. No part of this book may be reproduced in any form without permission in writing from the publisher. Please send bulk order requests to info@ninjalifehacks.tv

Paperback ISBN: 978-1-63731-666-5
Hardcover ISBN: 978-1-63731-668-9
eBook ISBN: 978-1-63731-667-2

Printed and bound in the USA.
NinjaLifeHacks.tv

Ninja Life Hacks®
by Mary Nhin

Social Ninja
A Book About Making Friends

Ninja Life Hacks
by Mary Nhin

I haven't always been this social and friendly. I used to be nervous and didn't know how to make friends.

Next, I remember to **stay** positive with my body language and comments while I'm listening.

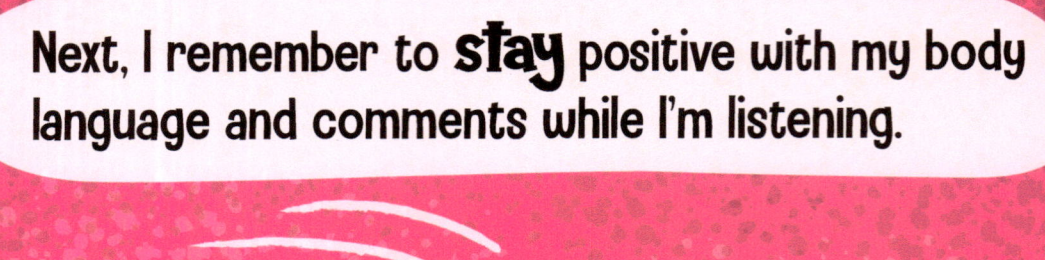

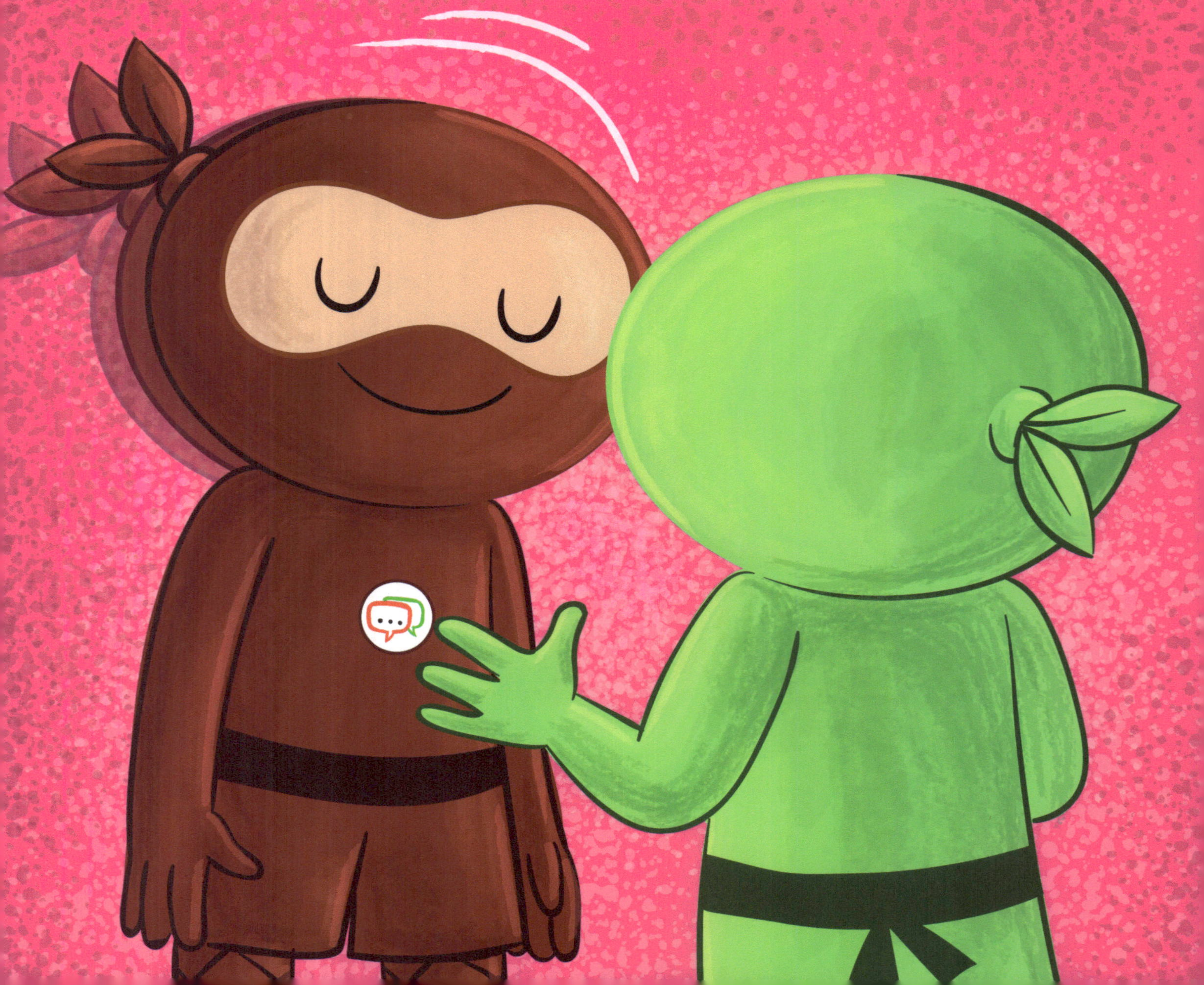

Finally, I **spot** any social cues like yawning or their eyes looking away. When someone does this, sometimes it means they're ready for the conversation to end, but we should never assume! It's best to ask, "Do you still have time to talk" or "Do you need to get going?"

Continue the learning with our fun lesson plans which include 3 Ss superpower skills practice, STEM activity, craft, and more! Visit ninjalifehacks.tv

 @marynhin @officialninjalifehacks
#NinjaLifeHacks

 Ninja Life Hacks

 Mary Nhin   Ninja Life Hacks

 @officialninjalifehacks